ENGLISH
COUNTRY CHURCHES

JOHN CURTIS

Text by Richard Ashby

SALMON

INTRODUCTION

The English country church is at the heart of its community. While our cathedrals show English architecture at its most sophisticated, it is the country church which shows the devotion and commitment of local people to what was for centuries, and is often still, the most important building in their town or village. They were built to the glory of God in profusion, primarily as places of worship; an expression of that common faith which over the centuries has become fragmented and today is in steep decline. But they were built also with pride by the local community and as an expression of their confidence in themselves. They wanted the best in their churches which over the centuries were added to, rebuilt, extended and beautified.

James *Chipping Campden, Gloucestershire*

But churches were also a source of rich controversy. At the Reformation and during the period of Cromwell's Commonwealth they were subject to much destruction and change to fit them for the new and different worship of the reformed Church of England. And then came the Victorians with their ideas of what a Christian church should be and many were subject to drastic restorations. So what we see today is a remarkable history in stone of the lives and aspirations of many centuries. It is also important to remember the purpose for which these churches were built. Here 'prayer is made valid' says the poet T S Eliot, and the walls of these churches are infused with the hopes and fears, the joys and the sorrows of the people who loved them and indeed still do.

HOLY TRINITY, LONG MELFORD
Suffolk

Wool was important in East Anglia and the prosperity it brought is reflected in the churches of the area. This is one of England's most glorious. It dates almost entirely from the end of the 15th century, the peak period of English church architecture, though the tower is a 20th century replacement. The church is built largely of the local flint; stone being scarce and thus expensive. Before the Reformation the walls and ceilings would have been brightly painted and all the windows filled with coloured glass. Only one medieval window survives in which there is a portrait of Elizabeth Talbot, said to have been used as the model for John Tenniel's drawing of the Duchess in *Alice in Wonderland*.

ST MARY AND ST DAVID, KILPECK
Herefordshire

Kilpeck is the most perfect and complete of this country's Norman churches. The famous carvings, executed in the unusually hard red sandstone of which the church is built, are still fresh and vigorous. Here the medieval imagination runs riot with images of animals, mythical creatures and biblical scenes.

ST JOHN THE BAPTIST, INGLESHAM
Wiltshire

Unlike so many other churches, Inglesham escaped the Victorian restorers who believed th the only true architecture for Christian worsh was that of the 14th century. William Morris intervened and so the 19th century repairs to the church preserved the furnishings and decorations which include centuries of wall-paintings. Although no longer used for regula services, the church is still consecrated and in the care of the Churches Conservation Trust.

ST MICHAEL, DUNTISBOURNE ROUS
Gloucestershir

On a hillside on the remote Cotswolds north o Cirencester is this little church with its Saxo nave and Norman chancel, underneath whic there is a little crypt chapel. Unlike so man churches in this wool-rich area, this one ha remained much as it was when first buil except for the small Tudor saddleback towe

ST MARY, WHITBY *North Yorkshire*

Captain Cook sailed from Whitby on his voyages of discovery and it is the landing place of Count Dracula in Bram Stoker's famous story. It was at Whitby that the ancient Celtic church of Britain met in synod with the later evangelists who came from Rome and agreed to the unification of the two rival Christian traditions. The church, solid and low, as if sheltering from the winds, stands on the cliff edge high above the town next to the remains of St Hilda's Abbey and is reached by a long climb up 199 stone steps. It looks out over the sea which brought life and death to its parishioners, and still does. Inside, it is a gem of unrestored Georgian, full of galleries and box pews, many of which lead into each other as a sort of maze, but all designed to give an uninterrupted view of the pulpit which dominates the interior.

ST PETER-ON-THE-WALL BRADWELL-ON-SEA *Essex*

Churches surviving from Saxon times are rare; the Norman invaders were usually keen to sweep away anything remaining of the previous era. This survivor may be the oldest in England. It was built sometime in the 7th century on the foundations of the main gateway (hence its dedication) and using brick and tiles from the Roman fort of Othona.

ST MARY THE VIRGIN, OARE *Somerset*
R D Blackmore was the grandson of the
Rector of Oare. In *Lorna Doone*, the only
novel for which he is remembered, the
heroine is shot at the altar steps in
this church at her wedding.

NEWLANDS *Cumbria*

The Newlands Valley lies south-west
of Keswick in the Lake District, rather
away from the haunts of mass tourism.
The little chapel, with its school room,
was built to serve the isolated farming
and mining communities of the area.
The earliest record, a map of 1576,
shows a chapel here but the building
may be even older, although it had to
be substantially rebuilt in 1843 and
has been restored several times since.
Inside there is an unusual lectern
with a sandstone plinth; removing the
wooden top transforms it into a font
for baptisms. Wordsworth walked this
valley with his sister in the spring of
1846 and, glimpsing the whitewashed
church through the trees, was inspired
to write about it in his poem *To May*.
The chapel unusually has no dedication

ST MARY, ABBEY DORE *Herefordshire*

Situated at the end of the 'Golden Valley' in a remote part of Herefordshire on the edge of Wales, this church is what is left of a 12th century Cistercian abbey; the claustral buildings have mostly gone, as has the nave. The remaining chancel, crossing and transepts have a wonderful majesty about them and are built in the Early English style with tall lancet windows. The abbey was suppressed in 1535 and became a ruin, fit for nothing better than the sheltering of cattle. The great church was rescued a hundred years later by the local Scudamore family who restored it, it is said, to make amends for profiting from its original destruction. They built a new tower and furnished the church with wonderful woodwork which included a new roof and a fine oak screen at the entrance to the chancel.

CHURCH OF THE GOOD SHEPHERD LULLINGTON *East Sussex*

This church was built in the 13th century on a hill above the Cuckmere Valley in the South Downs. Why only the chancel of the original building survives is not known. Tradition says that most was destroyed in Cromwell's time.

ST JOHN, SHOBDON *Herefordshire*

In Georgian times the original Norman church here was swept away and replaced by this extraordinary building with its blue and whit plasterwork, ogee arches, triple decker pulpit and fantastic bench ends. It looks more like a elaborate wedding cake than a church! The Norman font survives, however, returned afte serving as a garden ornament, and much of th richly carved interior of the original church was formed into a folly, still standing nearby.

ST MARY THE VIRGIN, HOLY ISLAND
Northumberlan

St Aidan came to this lonely an windswept spot to establish his monastery o Lindisfarne in 635 AD. The island is cut of from the mainland twice a day, so providin the isolation needed by the monks. Alongsid the monastery, the parish church serve the needs of the local fishing communit

T OSWALD, LOWER PEOVER *Cheshire*
'he village name comes from the Saxon for
'parkling stream' and is pronounced 'Peever'.
's church, dating from 1269, is largely
onstructed from oak. A 19th century poem,
'amed on the west wall inside, is a tribute
) the tree which contributed so much, both
) the architecture of this church and to
England's Walls', the ships of England's
aval forces.

'alk not of Syrian cedar,
Jor yet of foreign pine,
nd mention not the timber
Df any other clime.
ut see our native oak
1 noble grandeur stand,
'he dread of every sea,
'he glory of our land.

here is much good woodwork, some of it
edieval, and Jacobean box pews.

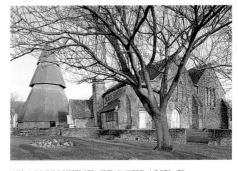

ST AUGUSTINE, BROOKLAND *Kent*
The 13th century wood frame of this most
unusual detached bell tower is covered in
wooden shingles. The dedication links the
church to the earliest days of Christianity in
England when St Augustine established his
mission at Canterbury not far away. There is
another link with the mother church of
England in the medieval wall-painting of the
martyrdom of Thomas à Becket, uncovered
during restorations in the 1960s.

ST CLEMENT, OLD ROMNEY *Kent*

The ancient port of Old Romney was left high and dry when the surrounding marshes were drained. The inhabitants moved to the new port at New Romney leaving the church isolated in a meadow. It dates from Norman times but inside, it is a haven of restrained Georgian 18th century fittings, painted a cool pink.

ST MARY, SOMPTING *West Sussex*

The distinctive Saxon tower of Sompting church, on the slope of the South Downs, is the only remaining one of its type in England. It is capped with a 'Rhenish Helm', typical of towers in the Rhineland designed to stop the snow from accumulating on the roof.

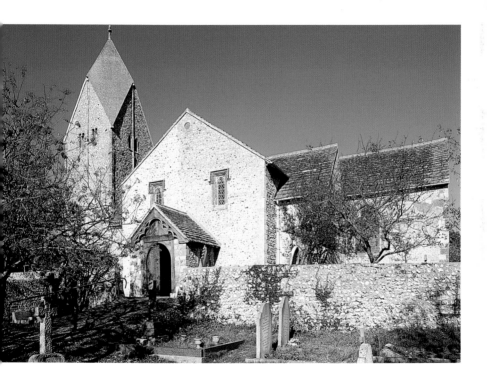

ST GILES, STOKE POGES
Buckinghamshire

In the quiet churchyard of this little church in the Chilterns, by his mother's tomb, the poet Thomas Gray wrote one of the most famous poems in the English language, his *Elegy Written in a Country Churchyard*. The lines beginning 'The curfew tolls the knell of passing day…' are ingrained in the English cultural memory.

ST MARY THE VIRGIN, INGESTRE
Staffordshire

Sir Christopher Wren is famous for his rebuilding of St Paul's Cathedral and many parish churches in London after the Great Fire of 1666, but this is his only church outside the city. It was consecrated in 1677 by the bishop who baptised a child and conducted a wedding and a funeral all on the same day.

ST MARY, FOTHERINGAY
Northamptonshire

Fotheringay will forever be associated with the unhappy Mary Queen of Scots beheaded on the orders of her rival Elizabeth I in the nearby castle. The castle has gone, only the earthworks are left. The great early 15th century collegiate church remains, although foreshortened by the demolition of its choir after the Reformation when the chantries were suppressed. The octagon tower is an important Northamptonshire landmark. The church was established by Edmund Plantagenet, the founder of the House of York, but it was his son, Edmund, Duke of York, who built the church we see today. Edmund was killed at Agincourt and his tomb, once in the now demolished choir was brought inside on the orders of Elizabeth.

ST MARGARET, HALES *Norfolk*

This thatched Norman church, with its Saxon chancel, stands alone in the Norfolk countryside. It has richly-carved doorways and inside, a medieval painting of St James the Great, the patron saint of pilgrims. Perhaps pilgrims on their way to Walsingham may have stopped here?

ST MARY AND ST HARDULPH, BREEDON ON THE HILL

Leicestershire

The church stands prominently on its hill and is a landmark to travellers on the busy A42 not far away. Over the centuries the hill has been quarried away and the church now stands on the edge of a cliff. It is an ancient Christian and pre-Christian site and a monastery, founded here in the 7th century, was important enough to be noted in the Anglo-Saxon Chronicles and by the Venerable Bede. The church is all that remains of a much larger building; the 12th century nave and the monastic buildings having been destroyed after the Reformation, leaving only the tower and the 13th century chancel. It has been much restored since, although its essential Norman character remains, and there are some fine surviving Saxon carvings inside.

ST ENODOC, TREBETHERICK *Cornwall*
By the 19th century this church was being engulfed by the surrounding sand dunes and the vicar had to be lowered into it through a hole in the roof. It was restored in 1864 and immortalised in John Betjeman's poem *Sunday Afternoon Service in St Enodoc Church*. The Poet Laureate knew the area well and is buried in the churchyard.

ST LAURENCE, BRADFORD-ON-AVON
Wiltshire

The near-complete Saxon church of
St Laurence was once lost to view, being used
as a school and a cottage and entirely
surrounded by other buildings. In the 19th
century the local vicar began to investigate
the history of the building and, recognising i
as an early church from two carved angels, se
about its restoration.

ST BUENO or ST CULBONE, CULBONE
Somerse

This tiny church on the edge of Exmoor, i
reached along a mile and a half track from
the nearest road. Culbone is a corruptio
of the Celtic 'Kil Buen' or church of St Beun
who is second in importance only to St Davi
in Wales. It is said that St Michael knocke
the spire off nearby Porlock church with
bolt of lightning and brought it here

ST MICHAEL, BRENTOR *Devon*

St Michael, the Archangel, led the armies of heaven to defeat the Devil. Nowhere would a church dedicated to him seem more necessary in an age of faith and superstition than on this outcrop of an extinct volcano in the wilds of Dartmoor where the presence of the Devil must have seemed very real.

ST MICHAEL with ST MARY MELBOURNE *Derbyshire*

There is a gallery around the four sides of the church giving access to a former upper chancel, the outline of which can clearly be seen on the tower. This suggests that it was built as a royal church for Henry I who had a manor nearby. It is a church of great power, with massive Norman columns and arches. Amongst the rich carving is the 'Melbourne cat' grinning across the chancel at a dog having its tail pulled!

ST MATTHEW, NORMANTON *Rutland*

Rutland Water is one of the largest man-made reservoirs in Europe. In the middle is this extraordinary survivor. The church is comparatively recent, being built in 1826 in the classical style. Before the reservoir was flooded the floor level of the church was raised and a causeway built. It now houses an exhibition on the building of the reservoir.

ST ANDREW, GREENSTED *Essex*

Early Christian churches in England were built of wood from the forests which covered the land and wooden walls survive in this church in rural Essex. It is at least a thousand years old, perhaps older; the oldest wooden-walled church in the world. The nave is made from oak logs, split lengthwise. The wooden shingled tower is 17th century.

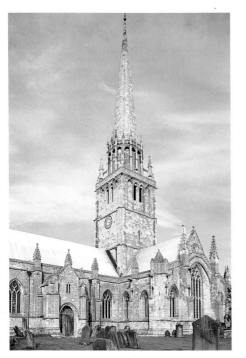

ST PATRICK, PATRINGTON *Yorkshire*

Known as 'The Queen of Holderness' this church's spire is visible from many miles away across the flat landscape of East Yorkshire beyond Kingston upon Hull. It is 14th century and has the scale of a small cathedral, reflecting the prosperity of this agricultural area. There is a fine 15th century Easter Sepulchre, showing Christ rising from the tomb and the sleeping soldiers.

Published in Great Britain by J. Salmon Ltd., Sevenoaks, Kent TN13 1BB. Telephone 01732 452381.
Email enquiries@jsalmon.co.uk
Design by John Curtis. Text and photographs © John Curtis
ISBN 1-902842-63-4   Printed in Italy © 2005

Title page photograph: St Mary, Lastingham *North Yorkshire*
Front cover photograph: St Bartholomew, Fingest *Buckinghamshire*
Back cover photograph: St. Just, St. Just in Roseland *Cornwall*